Writing for the Web

James Lowery

ISBN:1518894143
ISBN-13: 978-1518894145

DEDICATION

For everyone who knows why apostrophes matter and remember to put them there.

CONTENTS

Introduction: Writing for the Web

As marketers we have an array of tools at our disposal. Different media give us the opportunity to touch the senses of our audience. A striking picture or a piece of music can create a powerful emotional response in people and influence their opinion. Words are different. Less visceral, subtler, words have more potential as a marketing tool. Rather than giving us access to the senses of a person they give us access to their imagination.

Writing gives us the ability to create a story with the reader at the centre. A picture might be worth a thousand words, but the right words, used in the right way, and presented to the right person are priceless.

That's the hard part: Choosing those right words. Those phrases that create desire, paint the picture that we want them to and evoke the right response in our reader.

The web has made us all into writers – status updates, blogs mean that individuals we all write for a wider audience than previous generations. With email, chat, and SMS we communicate individually in writing more than any of the great writers of the past.

Such unfettered access to an audience should mean that we're better writers than at any time in history. But when you read a poorly structured, rambling blog post or a grammatically nonsensical email it doesn't feel that way.

In the past, writing was special, it was a privilege to be able to commit words to paper in the knowledge they would be treasured. These days, most of what we write is pretty disposable.

But.

There are times when good writing matters. Sometimes, a carelessly tossed off piece of prose isn't enough. In business, poor writing undermines the confidence of the reader. It harms sales. In the online arena, where your competitors are no more than a click away, a misspelling or a grocer's apostrophe might be enough to drive a potential buyer to the next search result.

A well thought out, well written web page or email has a lot of power. If you spend the time to consider the purpose of a page: it's audience, and objective, then it will be more engaging, interesting, and ultimately successful.

This book is about writing. Mainly for the web. It's not intended to be exhaustive, or overwhelming. It's not about the intricacies of grammar (although if you're a writer, it makes sense to have an understanding of what goes where), it's about the thought process you should include when you write, and the importance of getting writing right.

General Writing Tips

Let's get one thing clear before we start:

Writing isn't easy.

Thankfully, there are many things that you can do to make yourself into a better and more consistent writer. You might never find yourself in a position where you're entirely comfortable with writing – that blank page will always be a teeny bit daunting – but you can do a lot to make writing easier.

Preparing to Write

Writing requires preparation and time. The more of both you give yourself, the better your work will be. Usually.

Actual writing – putting words on a page or a screen – is only one part of the process of creating content. It's probably not even the most important part.

Plan

This is my approach to writing:

It's not just a case of writing a piece and hitting publish. You want to ensure that it is complete and works for the reader.

At every stage in the writing process, it's important to be as efficient as possible. Research is important, because it ensures that you include the right information for readers, but if you haven't set limits on the scope of what you're writing in the outline, then you can end up doing more work than you need to. Also, you might add a lot of stuff that's interesting, but irrelevant.

You need to set time aside to do your work well.

That means that you need to be pretty disciplined about structuring your working day to allow yourself enough space to ensure that your writing is comprehensive enough (research), and refined enough to provide your readers with what they want. If you leave out stages in this process, you will finish up with something sub-standard.

Read. A lot.

As Stephen King said:

> *If you don't have time to read, you don't have the time — or the tools — to write. Simple as that.*

Reading other people's work is hugely important in your development as a writer. If you don't expose yourself to different styles and different kinds of writing, then you will forever confine yourself to a very narrow set of skills.

Writing styles are often very specific to the topic and medium that you're writing for. A web page is not the same as a novel, and a tweet is not the same as an email.

Something to remember:

If you want to be a better writer, you need to read things twice:

- *Once as a member of the audience who the piece has been written for.*
- *Once in a critical way to understand how the writer has constructed the text.*

By reading the text in a critical way, you become more aware of how the piece has been written to achieve a goal. Look at the language that's been used, and the way the paragraphs are constructed. Think about the way ideas are introduced and expanded upon, and how the overall goal of the writing has been achieved.

Don't restrict yourself to only reading good things. You can learn just as much from a bad piece of writing as a good one. If something you read doesn't engage you properly as a reader, think about "why". What did the writer do wrong, or not do at all? Bad writing helps you improve your own work.

Find a Quiet Space

The actual act of writing is almost always a solitary activity. You might be in a group when you get inspired, or when you're planning or reviewing your writing, but for the most part, you'll be a more efficient writer if you find a quiet space and write alone.

You need to avoid distractions when you're writing. An interruption will slow you down, but it might also result in you missing something or leaving a sentence unfinished.

If you're working in an office where there's a lot of fussing about and no opportunity to hide away in a quiet corner, it's a good idea to adopt the universal symbol of "leave me alone":

Headphones

Even if you don't actually listen to music on them, most people will respect the fact that you don't want to be disturbed unless it's incredibly important.

Separate Writing and Editing

I can't stress how important it is to separate writing and editing and making them into distinct stages of your process. Hemingway summed up the difference like this:

Write drunk, edit sober.

It's good advice. When you're actively writing, it's easy to get lost in the prose. You get into a groove and get stuff done. It's not necessary to actually be drunk when you write. It's more a mind-set: be liberated, rather than cautious. Allow yourself to do the writing.

Editing is just as, if not more important than actually writing. Again, Hemingway:

The first draft of everything is shit.

Your first pass over the subject will have conflicting ideas, and will often contain a tonne of inconsistency. Editing gives you the opportunity to turn what you write into what you mean, and clothe your ideas in something sensible.

Some writers prefer their first draft to set the tone of what they're writing – it will include the turns of phrase that are important to the message, and the overall feel will be complete. Others prefer to focus on the structure and then flesh it out later with the right tone. There's no right way, try both, try neither, but avoid writing and editing together – you'll just end up with something that will be "right" but won't necessarily be coherent.

Enjoy Your Subject

Sometimes as a writer, you'll find yourself with a brief to write about something that's totally uninspiring to you. If you're not interested in what you're writing, it will show through to the reader. If you're bored, you'll bore them too, and they'll move on.

Over the years, I've had clients that were in industries that seemed so dull that I didn't think I'd be able to write 50 words about them, let alone 50 pages. The way I've always got around this is to look in more detail at the subject. The more you get involved in a topic, the more you learn, the more you learn, the more you realise there is to learn, and when you start to get into the habit of exploring, you'll find that it comes across in your writing.

Think about watching paint dry. That's pretty drab. But actually, there's a lot going on:

Think about the process of the paint drying. Sometimes it's a chemical reaction, but it can also happen through evaporation, or absorption. It's all dependent on the type of paint and the material that's been painted.

What about the colour of the paint? Does it remain consistent through the drying process? Why does that happen, why is it important?

What about the smell of paint: what causes it, is it dangerous, why does it give you a headache?

The more you dig into a topic, the more you learn, and usually, the more questions you have. If you're writing for a client on a topic that seems dull, think about what motivates the client to work in that industry.

Write for Your Audience

One of the most important goals of any piece of writing is to connect with a reader. Writing is about communication – sharing a piece of information in a way that the reader will appreciate fully and be able to act on. Whether you're informing a reader about something, or selling something to them, it's vitally important that you are able to put that information across in a way that they can understand fully.

One of the mistakes that a lot of writers make is that they write for themselves.

Why's that an issue?

People are different in a lot of ways, but one thing that we all have in common is that we think the most important person in the world is "me". Our perception of everything is coloured by our own experiences and personal preferences:

When we read something, we're often asking the question "what's in it for me?"

Over the past few years, social media has narrowed our perception of the world enormously:

We filter our exposure to ideas by following a small, selective group of people on Facebook and Twitter; we move away from broadcast TV toward YouTube Playlists and binge watching on Netflix; and we skip over things we're not interested in on TiVo. We have access to infinite amounts of information and culture, but all it serves to do is enable us to focus on the things we enjoy most.

Anyway, enough of the bleakness of the internet age.

What all this stuff means for a writer is they need to be even more in tune with what their readers want than ever before. Particularly on the web.

If your reader doesn't feel engaged by your content, they will skip onwards. So you need to be super sensitive about their needs and desires and write specifically for them.

Know Your Audience
Before you put pen to paper, (or pixel to screen), you need to think about who you are writing for, and understand what they want, what they want to read, and how they want to read it.

One of the greatest skills you need to have as a writer is empathy. Put yourself in the position of your reader, and know them.

If you're writing a page that's intended to a specific product, think about how it will impact on the reader. Why would they want it, what would they use it for, and what would convince them to choose to get it from you.

Know Their Triggers
Desire is a pretty complex emotion. There is a big difference between simply wanting it, and needing it. When you're writing a sales page, it will be much more effective if you know what will trigger desire for your product in the audience that's reading the page.

Think about the audience as a set of likes and dislikes and ambitions, and then consider the relationship that this creates with your product:

- *What interests them?*
- *What motivates them?*
- *What do they dislike?*
- *How do they want to feel?*

Ask yourself whether it's safe to generalise about your readers – are they all the same, or will your content need to encompass multiple triggers that will convince a reader to desire something.

In order to transform your reader from being interested to *wanting*, and ultimately to *needing*, you will need to show the product in a way that appeals to their deeper instincts. In many cases, this will boil down to:

- *This product will make other people view you in the way you want to be perceived*

Apple do this really well through the imagery and language they use to describe their products, but when you start to build emotional triggers into your writing that are tailored to your product and audience relationship, you'll find the ability to do the same.

Know Their Situation

There are a lot of ways to access content, so it's really vital to consider how a reader will engage with your writing. If you're writing a book, think about where your readers are likely to read it:

Are your audience young commuters who will read on a train journey. Does this mean that you need to write shorter self-contained chapters?

If you're writing for the web, consider whether your readers are likely to read on a mobile phone or a computer. Will they read at work when you need to make pieces shorter and focus on presenting information up front, or are they reading for leisure where you can be a bit more expansive.

If your audience are reading on a mobile device, does this mean that you need to use different language, or make pages shorter. How will the text render on different devices?

The more comfortable your reader feels about engaging with your content, the easier it is to make it successful. Take their situation into account with your structure and make it as comfy as possible for the reader.

Avoid Jargon

People are all pretty tribal and language reflects this. Particularly in business. Jargon – specialist language proliferates in organisations, especially those types of organisation which are in a technical field.

The big problem with jargon is that it isn't necessarily the language your customers are likely to use. As an example, a big UK retailer preferred to call laptop computers "notebooks". This should have been fine. After all, that's the proper name for the class of device, and also, for the most part, manufacturers tend to warn against resting a computer on your lap, because it doesn't usually allow enough air to get into the cooling system. That didn't matter to consumers. They called the devices laptops, and couldn't find what they were looking for on the retailer's website. Once they swallowed their corporate pride and switched to the commonly used term, they sold more.

Where possible, describe your products in the way that your customers do so that you appeal to what they want.

Keep Things Simple

Most of what we write is meant to be read and understood, so it makes sense to keep it as simple as possible.

You don't need to write at an idiot level, but you should write in a way that is clear, concise, and easily followed.

There's usually a purpose in writing – to take the reader from one idea to another (here's a product, here's why you should buy it). If you make the prose to complex, it becomes harder for the reader to appreciate what you want them to do. If they don't follow your guidance, they won't do what you want.

Clarity and simplicity come from careful editing. Make certain that you take the time to re-read and revise your writing before you publish to ensure that all points are explained and that the overall subject is clear.

Simplicity doesn't mean that you avoid depth, you should still be comprehensive.

Write for Comprehension

When you research who your main audience are, you can get an idea for the level of complexity in language that they can comfortably understand. There are a few different measures that you can use to compare your writing with the level that you would expect from your audience.

Readability statistics from Microsoft Word (or Google Docs) are a useful way of ensuring that you create content that matches the needs of your readers. A typical readability report looks like this:

Readability Statistics	? ✕
Counts	
Words	1,220
Characters	5,674
Paragraphs	45
Sentences	60
Averages	
Sentences per Paragraph	1.8
Words per Sentence	18.4
Characters per Word	4.5
Readability	
Flesch Reading Ease	66.5
Flesch-Kincaid Grade Level	8.4
	OK

The Flesch Reading Ease test score is based on how easy a piece of writing is to read. For a general adult audience, you would expect the score to be from 60-70. The Flesch-Kincaid Grade Level indicates the level of education under the American schooling system at which the content is comfortable.

Use readability statistics as a guide for how easy to understand your writing is. They're not a replacement for actual proof reading and editing.

Writing Web Pages

When people are online, they have different needs at different times: sometimes they're researching, relaxing, or looking for inspiration; at other times, they're in the market to buy something specific.

Depending on what a user is looking for at a particular time, they will be more receptive to different types of content. If you're managing a website's content strategy, it's useful to have a variety of different types of content that are suitable for the different readers you'll have. These usually fall into a number of categories:

- *Content Pages*
- *Navigational Pages*
- *Sales Pages*

Content pages might be blog posts, or information about your business. They play a part in the sales process, because they add reassurance to users about the wider facts of your business, but they typically don't convert directly.

Navigational Pages appear in the site and guide users through to deeper pages with specific content. On a retail website these might be actual category or department pages with lists of products, while on a website for a services business, they might be guides to a topic.

Sales Pages are where the magic happens. This is where your website promotes specific products and services, and where you have the opportunity to close a sale.

There are certain things that are true for all the different types of page:

- They need to engage the reader
- They need to show your business in a positive light
- They need to be well structured to provide information as quickly as possible

These days, you will probably also want to think about Search Engine Optimisation (SEO) as part of the process of writing web content. It's essential for users to be able to find your content online, and search is the dominant source of traffic. There's been a tendency for some writers to prioritise the process of getting the SEO right above getting the content right, and that can lead to some bad experiences for users.

Regardless of what kind of page you're writing for your website, you should always think about what the user wants from that page, and focus on that first. SEO comes later.

Outstanding Opening Paragraphs

Whether you're writing a web page, an email, or a novel, what you put in the first few lines can have a huge impact on how engaged your audience are. A strong opening that captures the reader's attention immediately can grab their attention immediately, and pull them into the content straight away.

If you have a specific objective with your writing – such as to sell a product or idea – getting the opening right will make all the difference with your level of success. So it makes sense to put the effort in, and work hard on grabbing your reader by the collar and exciting them from the start.

There are many different ways of opening a piece of writing. The best one for you will depend on a lot of things:

- *The type of content you're writing*
- *The purpose of your writing*
- *What your audience are expecting*
- *Who your audience are*

One thing to remember: What you write in that opening paragraph is essential in setting the scene for the rest of the piece, but it's also something that you need to follow through on. If your opening line is astonishingly brilliant, but the rest of what you write is a turgid mess, then you might as well not bother putting the effort in up front. Your first paragraph needs to set the scene. The rest of your writing needs to raise the bar even higher.

Here are some tips on the best ways to grab the attention of your audience at the start of your writing.

Open with a question

Why would you start a piece of writing with a question?

Well, for a start, it's a great way of immediately bringing your reader into the text. By asking a question, you are able to make them think of a particular set of circumstances that you can then use to your advantage in the rest of what you're writing.

If you're writing a sales page, opening with a question is a really powerful tool that allows you to capture the reader's attention quickly and make them start thinking about the benefits of what you're selling right at the start of the page. There's no messing about: it's efficient and simple:

- *Wouldn't it be great to win the lottery?*

Of course, the main thing about opening with a question is that you need to provide an answer that allows you to segue into the rest of the page and sell your products. A sales page is essentially a very structured piece of writing that needs to follow a specific course, so whatever question you ask needs to allow only one possible answer.

Your reader needs to answer the question exactly as you intend, otherwise you're immediately in conflict. If you're opening with a question, keep it simple, rhetorical, and ideally, make it something where the only possible answer is "yes" so that you get your reader in the right habit immediately:

- *Do you value great customer service?*
- *Isn't it time you got the promotion you deserve?*
- *Don't you think it's great when you get time to relax?*

An alternative to a question that can work well too is a simple statement – one that a reader is likely to agree with. This works in the same way of building rapport, but is a bit subtler:

- *We all value our time.*
- *There's nothing worse than buying something that doesn't work.*
- *If you're anything like me, you probably want to spend more time with your family.*

If you pitch your question or statement right, you'll find that the overall power of your writing is much higher, and you'll get exactly what you want.

Start with a quote

My father always said: "if you want people to look up to you, use the words of someone they respect".

And that sums up the value of opening a piece of writing with a quote from someone else.

If you pick the right quote, from the right person, you create a very powerful opening to your writing because you borrow the authority and respect that the originator of the quote has. In fact, you don't necessarily need to use the words of a famous person. In the opening of this section, I used my father. I could have used my mother, or a grandparent for the same effect.

Making a decision can be stressful, and what we often need is reassurance that we're doing the right thing. A quote from an authority figure helps to give us that reassurance.

Some things to think about:

If you're going to use a celebrity, make sure they're dead. If you pick someone who is alive, then you run the risk of making it look as though you're getting an endorsement that is dishonest. Aside from not suing you (which is a good thing), historic figures tend to have a lot more authority.

Avoid anyone who has negative associations from your audience. You might think a quote from Hitler is a good fit. Trust me, it isn't. Ever.

Shock Your Audience

A high impact opening to any piece of writing will get your reader to sit up and take notice. It is a fairly common tactic in sales writing to present a statistic at the start of the pitch that is then followed up in the rest of the piece.

There are a number of ways of creating that moment of surprise.

Sometimes these use the same tactics above, but with a fairly extreme question or quote:

- *90% of businesses fail in their first year. Will Yours?*
- *Without Disaster Recovery, your business could be dead in the water tomorrow.*
- *A recently enacted law means that you need to take action now*

if you're using the shock opening tactic, there are some things to think about:

- *It needs to jar with the subject or title of the email or document, but share a theme*
- *It needs to be verifiable*
- *It needs to be answered by the rest of your piece of writing*

On an email, if your opening "shock" statement doesn't follow on from the theme of the title that you used to encourage a user to open it, then you'll lose them immediately. if the rest of the document doesn't provide reassurance or answer the statement, then again, you'll simply leave the reader feeling unfulfilled and lose their attention.

Provide Your Conclusions Up Front

People are generally time poor – especially business people, so it's vitally important that you provide them with the simplest way of getting the message from your writing.

Whether you're presenting a lengthy proposal, or a short email, it's wise to provide your conclusions at the beginning in the form of an executive summary along with notes about the next steps that the reader needs to take.

For example, if you're proposing a particular service, state exactly what the projected outcomes and costs are and encourage the reader to follow through the document to get the full detail to help them make a decision.

In most cases, if you're presenting conclusions up front, it's better to give an overview in writing and then summarise again using a list of bullet points to reinforce what you're offering to the reader:

Hi Geoff

Happy to provide you with more information about how we'll deliver this service for your business to help you achieve 150% year on year sales growth for the ongoing fee of £2,000 per month:

- ○ *Ongoing customer contact services*
- ○ *150% Annual Sales Growth*
- ○ *£2,000 Monthly fee*

Don't overload the introduction with too much information – it's should be a brief executive summary of outcomes rather than actions - that's what the body of the writing is for.

Writing with SEO in Mind

If you're writing for the web, it's a good idea to take Search Engine Optimisation into account. Google and other search engines rank pages based on a number of on page factors that focus on the relevance of that page to the query a user has entered. Most of the time, people search with a short phrase which gets referred to as a "keyword".

Writing with SEO in mind shouldn't mean subverting the meaning of your text to solely focus on rules around how frequently a keyword appears in the copy, or forcing that keyword to appear in the text where it shouldn't. All it really requires is a bit of thought into the mind of a reader, and a review of your pages to see whether they are in line with what search engines want.

When you're writing a web page and you take into account SEO, there are a few areas that you'll want to consider in order to make the page as relevant as possible without detracting from user experience. In fact, these days, user experience is one of the most important ranking factors that Google have. They want to serve the best possible answers to a user's question, and this generally means promoting pages which are comprehensive in answering a subject.

It's important to ensure that your website contains answers to the different questions that a potential customer might ask, and also that the overall structure of your site broadly reflects the journey that the user will take when researching and buying.

Choose the Right Keywords

The process of selecting keywords for a web page can seem daunting. But it's really not. For the most part, your customers will behave exactly as you would yourself when searching for something. People behave differently depending on what stage of the buying process they're at. When they first start researching, they might look for something fairly general:

- *Mobile Phone*

As they get closer to making their decision, they're likely to search for something more specific:

- *Samsung Galaxy S6 Edge*

When you're doing research into the types of keyword that people use, it's handy to have access to a tool that will tell you roughly how many times a month people search for the keywords that you want to target.

There are a few tools on the market like SEMRush and SearchMetrics that provide estimates of search volume. If a phrase has a very large number of monthly searches, then it might not be prudent to target it – high volume means high competitiveness. Similarly, if a phrase only gets one or two searches each month, the effort you go to in writing the content may never be rewarded.

Prioritise based on potential value, and competitiveness. If you're doing SEO for your website, be realistic about who you are able to compete with. If the search results for the keywords you want to target are filled with Amazon, eBay, Wikipedia, and other highly authoritative sites, it's going to be really tough to get visitors.

Use Different Keyword Variations

Google and Bing are highly advanced when it comes to understanding text and the relationships between words. They are able to recognise that the following two phrases mean broadly the same thing:

- *Cheap Hotel Rooms New York*
- *Low Cost Places to Stay, New York*

When you're writing a web page and you want to perform well in the search results, it's a good idea to make your content comprehensive so that you cover off multiple variations in the body text. This has two main advantages:

- *It makes the text more readable and natural*
- *It allows you to gain traffic from a wider range of terms*

In addition to the above, a page with a broader range of terms is actually more appealing to search engines. SEO has a bad reputation when it comes to content. A lot of content that's written with just organic rankings in mind is really, really bad. It tends to be stilted and forced, and quite often says very little beyond repeating a keyword or phrase over and over again without really adding much of value. Google have taken steps to address this through a number of major updates which focus on so-called thin content. As a result, content with a broad base offers you a better chance of ranking.

Be Comprehensive

People use search engines to find information. It's a simple thing to bear in mind when it comes to SEO. Make your pages comprehensive about a particular subject. Write enough to answer the question that a user has in mind.

When a user is searching for something broad like "Hotels in Dubai", there are two concepts in their search:

- *Hotels*
- *Dubai*

Search engines have databases of billions of pages, and recognise that there are a lot of different topics that should be covered in a page based on these concepts. A user too would expect the page to have information about the following in order to help them make a decision:

- *Dubai as a city and destination*
  - *Things to do in Dubai*
  - *Attractions in Dubai and their locations relative to hotels*
- *Hotels in Dubai*
  - *Descriptions*
  - *Information about rates*
  - *Recommendations*

If you were to put this information into a Venn diagram it might look like this:

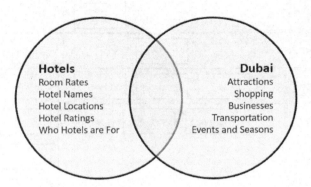

By covering the information a reader needs and expects, you're more likely to provide the information that a search engine identifies as being important and comprehensive.

A page that targets a broad term should be ... broad. As you move to more specific information, it needs to be more focused in the information that's provided. A generic page should provide enough information for a user to move to the next step in their buying process.

Structure Your Page

Content needs structure. When you write a page you need to make it simple for readers (and search engines) to understand the information you provide and give it context. Break the content into sections and introduce each section with a brief paragraph that summarises what follows. Allow your readers to scan through the content to find the bits that they're most interested in.

HTML provides a structure for documents that includes multiple headings. Using these properly gives search engines the additional information about what parts of the page are most important by creating a simple tree structure that can be interpreted by machines:

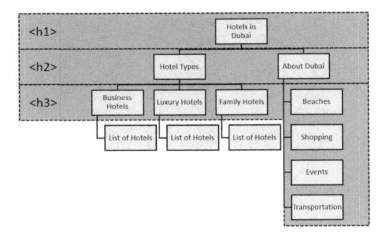

Using this type of clear structure allows you to be consistent in the depth of information that you provide on your pages and ultimately provide users with a more in depth experience on your site which should help to convince them to move onto the next stage in their buying process.

Page Titles and Meta Descriptions

When it comes to search, before a reader gets to your website they get a sneak preview in the form of the page title and meta descriptions for your pages which the search engines generally show in their results:

Amazon.com - Official Site — Title
www.amazon.com ▾
Online shopping from the earth's biggest selection of books, magazines, music, DVDs, videos, electronics, computers, software, apparel & accessories, shoes, jewelry ... — Meta Description

A thoughtfully composed, impactful title and meta description for your web page can make a big difference to how many people click through to your website from search, and as a result, it's worth investing the time and effort into making them as effective as possible.

Keep it Short

If your title or description is too long, then it won't be fully displayed in the search results. Google don't place a limit on the number of characters you can use, rather the number of pixels that those characters can take up – although it generally works out that 65 characters is the maximum length.

This does not allow many words. In fact: it gives you this many.

When it comes to the Meta Description, you've got a bit more room. Again, you are limited by pixels, but it works out on average at 160 characters. This many.

You don't need to use all of the space at your disposal, but discipline is essential in getting your message across in a limited space. More so when you're writing a commercial page, and you want to encourage the click as quickly as possible, and stand out from the competition.

Include the Necessary Information

We talked above about fitting things into the limited space available for the Title and Meta Description on your pages, but what do you really need to get in there?

- *What the page is about*
- *Your company name*
- *An explicit request for them to click through*

All of those things are very important, but if everyone's doing just that, then everyone will be pretty much the same. When I'm listing out the requirements for the Meta Description for a client's page, I always include one other thing:

- *Your USP – why the reader should click on your business*

This USP might be as simple as a price, but it might also be an indicator of what your brand is all about:

Buy your stuff from us today, and find out why 100% of our customers are still with us after 5 years. Click here to find out more.

The biggest selection of products anywhere? Absolutely, but that's not what makes us special. Check out our offers!

A lot of people treat their titles and descriptions as an afterthought. Treat them as an advert and apply the same love and attention to them as you would any piece of marketing material and you'll soon find that they deliver better results.

Intrigue your reader

Think about what might make a reader click through to your page.

The most effective way of encouraging a deeper level of engagement from your listing in the search results is to ask a question or a use a tease statement to lead the reader through to the page:

- *What's the secret of great looking hair?*
- *How do you know if he loves you?*
- *We never expected 4GB to be enough to run Windows 10. Find out why.*

If you're planning to use a question to get readers to click through, it's incredibly important to build the answer into the page structure. A question in your "advert" can be a great lead into a sales page, especially if you layer more intrigue on top through your writing.

A couple of things to be careful of:

- *Don't ask a question that the reader can answer without clicking through to your page*
  - *If you do, they won't*
- *Don't give the answer away on the first line*
  - *You're giving the reader an excuse to click away immediately.*

Use Your Brand

A company's brand is one of its most powerful assets. It can make the difference to a user having enough faith in your business to click through to your site. As such, focus on how you can present it to the reader effectively along with your key differentiator.

Most of the time, branding seems pretty lazy – writers will simply add the brand name to the title and probably squeeze it into the description.

You can do better.

If you have a brand that people will recognise, and even local businesses may achieve this, put it where a user will see it.

One of the most important parts of building an SEO campaign is to encourage people to click through to your site at the point where they're ready to buy. You need to make them aware of your business name from the moment they start searching, so that they get to the point where their internal monologue says something like:

- *I want to buy this product from Company X, because I trust them with my money.*

Be Different

For the most part, only about 1 in 3 people click on a result when they search. The rest get the information they need from the search results page, or simply decide that none of the sites they see is right for them.

Also, when you look at a standard set of search results, all of the sites are presented in the same way. We're conditioned to click on the top one, because the search engine's algorithms are designed to return the most relevant answer at the top.

If you want to break out of that trap, you need to stand out from the crowd, and the best way of doing that is to pay a visit to the search results page you want to target, and do something different to what's already there.

You might achieve that by composing a killer question, or presenting an eye catching price in your description, but sometimes it can be as simple as just structuring your page title slightly differently:

- *Hotels in New York | Company A*
- *Hotels in New York | Company B*
- *Hotels in New York | Company C*
- *Hotels in New York | Company D*
- *Hotels in New York | Company E*
- *Hotels in New York | Company F*

- *Company G >> Hotels in New York*
- *Hotels in New York | Company H*
- *Hotels in New York | Company I*
- *Hotels in New York | Company J*

A small difference can be all it takes to catch the eye and get more clicks than you might if you followed the herd.

Use Your Data

Google provide information through Search Console about click through rates from the search results, and you can analyse this at either a page level, or alternatively at a keyword level. Use this data to see which pages perform better or worse compared to average Click Through Rate (CTR) across your whole site.

If you're doing better on one page than another, look at what's made the difference, and then try and replicate that elsewhere on the site. This should be something that you're testing all the time, not just as a one off. The more experiments you run, the more data you have, and the more you'll be able to observe trends and find what works well.

From position 7 in a search results page, you get about 1% of the clicks, but more importantly, at position 7, the chances are that the person searching will have already looked at your competitors. Standing out could be enough to make a big difference in your CTR, which feeds back into the way Google rank sites, so you might also get longer term improvements in overall traffic.

What About Paid Search Advertising?

Most of the tips above also apply to your ad creation for AdWords and other pay per click services. The big difference is that you're much more limited in the number of characters you can use:

> **_25 letters in the heading_**
> _Just35characters.in/yourDisplayURL/_
> _Use 35 letters total for line one._
> _And the same number go in line two._

It requires enormous discipline to write great adverts in such a limited amount of space, but on the plus side, you can run loads of tests at the same time, and capture information about how your audience interact with different versions of the creative messaging and ultimately, what works to improve the click through rates.

Although the number of characters is even more limited than you'd get in your organic results, you can use the data you gather about what works well for your audience in your paid search activity to improve the performance of your titles and meta descriptions.

Persuasive Content for Sales Pages

Sometimes when you visit a store you'll encounter a really good salesperson who gets things absolutely right. From the moment they walk over to you to find out what you need until the moment you leave the store with more than you expected they sell to you. A good web page can do the same. If it's written well, uses persuasive language carefully, and is structured and presented to maximise the impact it has on you.

You come across persuasive content online quite a lot. Sales pages (that's proper sales pages, not a typical product page on an online retailer website) use persuasive content. As you read them, you find yourself gradually being won over as your various objections are cast aside.

By the time you've got to the bottom of the page, you're already reaching for your credit card.

If you're serious about selling through your website – rather than just having customers buy from you, you need to understand how persuasive content works, and how to use it properly.

Remove Distractions and Diversions

Jakob Nielsen talked about website visitors behaving like wild animals hunting for their next meal. If they can't find what they're looking for, and there are temptations to look elsewhere, they will. When you're creating a persuasive page where you want to sell something specific, you need to be certain that you're not leaving any other temptations on the page.

On a website there's normally lots of links to other places. You don't want these on a sales page. What you want is a straightforward experience for the user to be pulled towards a particular conclusion. simplify the page to ensure that once a person is on it, they are fully exposed to the content that you want them to read.

When you're presenting 3rd party information to back up your argument (more on this later), keep it in the page. offset images to one side and let the text flow around it as you guide the reader to the conclusion.

Don't put anything in the way of your smooth sales patter.

Keep the Writing Simple ... But Appropriate

It's easy enough to keep people on your page by giving them all the information they need to buy rather than making them look elsewhere. But sometimes, you can lose the customer simply by including words that are unfamiliar or unclear.

When you're writing a sales page, the last thing you want to do is to make the reader feel stupid. After all, an intelligent person would make the decision to buy!

The quickest way to alienate a reader is by using language that's too complex, or words that are so obscure that they need to pick up a dictionary to find out what they mean.

When you're drafting the page, use tools like Microsoft Word's readability scores to check what level of education the page is appropriate for. Always aim to make the page as easy to read as possible. Short sentences that can be understood first time are super effective.

Use common sense words to sell: don't endeavour to nonplus the peruser with your prodigious argot.

Sense of Urgency

want people to want to buy, you need to create a sense of
~~~~~, ~~ scarcity. Show throughout the page that the deal you've got
on the table is only available for a limited time or a limited number of
people.

> *That's why we're offering the whole pack – along with the
> additional free gifts to just 100 people who sign up by midnight
> tonight!*

Sales is about getting the commitment now, not next week, not
tomorrow, NOW.

Sure, you want the reader to "go away and think about it" - but the
thing you want them thinking about is what a great deal they've just
got, not whether they should sign up at all.

One thing to note about the urgency / scarcity approach is to be honest
about it. If you say the deal is only for the next 24 hours, ensure that
the price advertised goes up – but also give people who missed out on
the great deal the opportunity to get in touch to see if you can offer
them the same program that they've missed out on.

Own the Argument

Most of the time, when someone is in buying mode, they ask questions. If they don't get answers that satisfy them, they'll look elsewhere.

The key skill when writing persuasive content is to lead a potential customer to a specific question, and then provide them with an answer. Here's an example:

> After reading all that, you're probably wondering:
>
> **"how can they afford to sell at this low price?"**
>
> It's <u>simple</u>. We negotiate <u>better</u> deals with our suppliers – and pass those savings on to you!

The art of writing effective persuasive content is in steering the user to ask the questions you want them to ask. When you're planning your page, it's imperative that the first thing you do is structure the boxes that you want to tick off as you communicate the offer to customers, and then write answers which aim towards making the sale.

Text content isn't interactive; it doesn't adapt to how the reader interacts with it. You need to create the conditions for the reader to ask a question that you want to answer. If your content isn't focused enough to do that, then it won't work.

If you direct users to ask questions you haven't considered, they will ask them, you won't be able to answer them, and the customer will walk away without buying.

Use the Inverted Pyramid

Journalists use a structural system for writing called "the inverted pyramid". In this you make the most important point first, before providing additional background. An inverted pyramid is great for news stories because it allows the reader to get enough information from the opening paragraph to be able to understand what the story is about.

Sales pages are the same.

The first paragraph needs to be the conclusion:

You want to buy.

From that, you then use the rest of the page to make the case for the person to buy from you by describing the benefits of the product to the user.

By contrast, a non-persuasive page will usually start with the product, rather than a call to action, then list the features, before finishing with the call to action:

	Persuasive	Non-Persuasive
Start	Call To Action	Product
Beginning	Discussion of benefits	Discussion of features
End	Call to action	Call to action

Persuasive content maximises your opportunities to sell by asking for the business up-front, rather than leaving it to the end.

Focus on Benefits, not Features

When you're writing a page that sells a product, you shouldn't actually focus on selling the product. What you actually want to sell is the experience of ownership.

Take a look at a presentation by Apple. Their product launches are all about the benefits of ownership. They don't talk about the specifics of the processor inside the iPhone, just how smoothly it runs. They don't talk about the number of megapixels that the camera captures, they show you carefully chosen images that show how much fun you have when you're using it.

When you're writing your sales page, concentrate on the benefits. The ease of ownership, the simplicity of a feature, the pleasure that it will bring, not the mechanism by which it will achieve those ends.

Some people do buy based on the specs. So you need to include them for reference, they're important, but they're less important than the advantages.

Use Perceived Disadvantages as a Sales Tool

No product is entirely perfect, and no product is perfect for everyone.

The key to sell persuasively is not to gloss over a fault, but to sell it as an advantage.

For example, a lot of people drop their smartphone and crack the screen. Rather than using fragility as a potential objection, it becomes a feature and a benefit— you focus on the lightweight nature of the device. You use the low weight and materials as a sensory cue and benefit for the user "imagine how good it feels in your hand, you'll want to hold it tight."

Another example: a premium car costs a lot of money. Rather than using the expense as an objection, it becomes a feature and a benefit – you focus on the exclusivity of the car. You talk about how no corners have been cut and press the experience of being wrapped up in the leather. You show the reader that the experience of ownership is intensified by the exclusivity (no-one else can enjoy this) and the quality (you will enjoy this).

Assume the Sale

Both of the above tips lead to the same principal tenet of persuasive content: The assumed sale.

The person reading the copy is already a customer. You could call the process of writing this type of sales page "Reassuring Content".

Every word on the page is about making the buyer feel more comfortable about the purchase that they've already made. Write as though they've already made the decision to buy – talk about how good it feels to have made a decision, include references to the outcome that they've already chosen. The benefits of ownership that they're ready to enjoy.

Be Personal, Be Familiar

There are ways of personalising a web page so that it includes the name of the person, but these don't always work that well. Places like Amazon will include your name on the page, and it's a powerful tool for selling – we buy from people we trust, and someone who knows your name is generally someone you would trust.

But if you're running a sales page on a website and your user isn't logged in, then you're going to struggle to address them by their first name.

Instead, you need to write in a way that makes it look like you're more familiar with them:

> One of the biggest challenges that people like us face in our day to day lives is getting the right answer to a question. When we started our project, we wanted to find how we could help the people we like to get the same advantages as us and earn what they deserve.

We create an association with the reader by establishing a connection with them – a personal connection which suggests that we're familiar with their thoughts and feelings:

Just like you, we were nervous when we first saw the product, but we didn't need to, in fact, it's a bit silly to be worried about something so simple isn't it!

The more you can do to build rapport with the reader through addressing them directly, and using "we" inclusively, the more they will buy into what is being said.

Get Your Reader to Say Yes, *Yes*, YES!

Have you ever been on a sales course?

Of course you have. We've all been there!

When you are involved in face to face sales, you learn to look for "buying signals". A nod of the head, the customer leaning in closer to pay more attention. That's not as easy when someone is reading a web page. We need to work harder.

The most effective way of getting the big YES, is to get your reader in the habit of saying smaller yeses. The more you get them to agree with your points, the more likely they are to agree to click the button and buy.

When you read a really effective sales page, you'll find that there are low commitment questions throughout it that only a fool would say no to:

Are you ready to earn a little bit more money?

Can you imagine how good that will feel?

Do you really like it when someone says no?

As you write the page, you need to ensure that you're regularly asking questions that the reader will say yes to. That's the goal of persuasive content, and it's one of the most powerful tools around.

Don't Tease, Tantalise

Let's cut to the chase, persuasive content is a seduction, and purchase is the orgasm. The best orgasms are the ones where you've been held on the cusp of pleasure for the longest, because they're the ones which combine pleasure and relief in equal measure.

The most effective way of selling at the end of the page is to keep adding to the temptation throughout the page.

> *But wait, don't click buy just yet, here's something else that you'll really love – and it's part of the deal too!*

You want to intensify the pleasure that the reader is feeling, and their desire to buy. Think about the order in which you're adding value to the deal – make each bit better than the last.

Know When You've Won

The most important line on your page is the last. The point at which you've seduced, tempted, and tantalised your reader to make a purchase.

When you've got them to the brink, their hands shaking with desire, and their heart pounding, stop and give them what they want. The opportunity to say yes and taste what they've been waiting for.

Close the Deal

Once you've captured the reader's attention, increased their desire and teased them to the point where they're ready to click the button, you need to close the deal.

What's the simplest way of doing that?

Cutting the price at the last minute. Giving the reader a deal that they simply can't turn down, because it's even better than what you've given them already. Give them the feeling that by clicking the buy button they've won.

Helping Users Find their Way

Most of the time, a website is structured a bit like this:

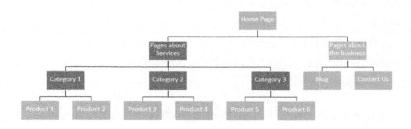

For many users, the most important part of their journey through your website is on the highlighted navigational pages. These are the pages which act as a link from your brand through to the pages where they buy.

If you go to a page on a typical retail website, it looks like this:

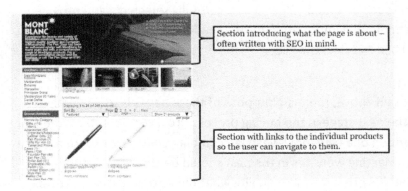

You'll notice that there's not much content on the page. That's important. Think about this page as being like the waiting area at a train station. It's not good to have people hanging around here too long – you want them to make their way to the products that they want to buy, so when you're putting together the page, it's useful to think about what will make the user continue on their journey.

Keep Category Pages Brief

Of all the pages on your website, these will be the ones with the least amount of actual copy.

For SEO reasons, you'll probably want to include a hundred words or so, but that's sufficient. The page simply needs to advise the readers what products are listed to enable them to decide whether this is the right place for them, and also contain a small amount of information about what makes your range special. You might open the page with something like this:

> Our **luxury hotels in New York** offer business travellers the perfect escape from the hectic streets of the city. We've carefully selected the best range of hotels in the heart of the city within walking distance of the main business centres, but also offering easy access to the nightlife and cultural highlights of the city.

In this paragraph we've highlighted what the page is focused on, added a little touch of added value "we've carefully selected", and provided some additional information for the reader about what criteria have been used to select the list.

Explain What Happens Next

As we said above, the main purpose of these pages is to push the user onto the next stage in the buying process. To a certain extent, the convention of a category level page combined with the experience of a user navigating websites in the past should be sufficient not to need this, but it's often useful to qualify what the next step is and provide some reassurance:

> All these hotels are available to book now for your chosen dates, and include the option of free cancellation if your plans change before you travel. Simply select the hotel that's best for your needs, and we'll do the rest.

Here we've made it clear that the products are available, added a degree of urgency "book now", and also provided some additional reassurance "the option of free cancellation", before stating precisely what the user needs to do next.

Inform the Choice

When someone is browsing a website, they're in the process of buying, but the longer they do it for, there is an increased risk of them moving off the site altogether. Too much choice isn't always a good thing.

Providing at a glance information about products is a useful way of funnelling the user towards making a decision. You might do this with a simple to understand set of icons, or a (very) brief summary of each product that encapsulates its difference in a few words:

- *Perfect for meetings*
- *Ideal for nightlife*
- *Overlooking Central Park*

When writing these snippets for products, think about what a user is most likely to value about the product and highlight that. Don't confuse them by having lots of similar descriptions.

Encourage the Click

In some ways, the most important words on a page are the call to action, and on a category page, they are vital. Depending on how hard your sell is, you will probably choose something in the following range:

- Find out more
- Click to explore
- Add to Basket
- Buy Now

Make certain that the phrase you've chosen is appropriate to the decision making process that the user is going through. A more considered (read "expensive") purchase is likely to benefit from a "find out more" type message on the link to the page, while something that's impulsive will be more like "buy it now".

Most Content Management Systems and ecommerce software will allow you to make changes to these buttons across the site so you can test out different versions to find out what works best for your customers and products.

Writing Truly Engaging Blog Posts

There's two kinds of blogs: the ones that people want to read, and the ones that nobody does.

The first kind are the ones which are written by people who have a genuine passion and enthusiasm for a subject, and are able to communicate that passion with their audience. They offer value and insight and encourage participation and further learning.

The second kind are the ones that a lot of businesses have on their website because an SEO guru told them it was a good idea. These blogs lack character, are light on insight and are generally ghost written by someone who's paid by the word, and has absolutely no incentive to develop a relationship with an audience.

There are plenty of reasons why you might blog: you might want to share your thoughts and experiences on a standalone blog or create a company blog to give you some additional engagement with your customers and promote new products. Whatever your reason for blogging, the process of writing a blog to attract and keep an audience is the same.

Care about your subject

If you don't have any enthusiasm about the subject of your blog it will come across in the quality of your writing, and your readers will pick up on that. Pretty soon, you won't have any readers.

There are no subjects that are completely dull. You can guarantee that no matter what the topic, there will be a passionate community celebrating it somewhere in the depths of the internet.

Not being passionate about something isn't a crime, but you won't get far along the audience building road unless you are. The key to getting enthusiasm with a dull topic is **an angle**. The concept of air powered machine tools might not be terribly interesting, but the stories of people who use them probably are.

If you're working on a corporate blog, writing about **end users** and **outcomes** can be a far more powerful marketing tool than writing endless posts about your products.

Do the research
You don't need to absolutely everything about your subject; you just need to know a little bit more than your readers.

People read blogs for two reasons:

- To be entertained
- To be **educated**

They don't visit (or recommend) blogs that bored them to tears with a load of things they already knew. If you're enthusiastic about something, you'll generally find it easier to entertain your reader, but unless you're also knowledgeable, you won't keep them on the page much beyond the first paragraph.

When you're writing a blog post, **research is essential**. If you're promoting a product or idea, make sure you know about what the product is. You don't need to be an expert, but you need to be comprehensive. Spend time reading before you write a blog post, and you'll find that not only is it easier to write, it's also better and more valuable to readers too.

Stand Out
The problem with blogs is that there's too many of them. With no barrier to entry (aside from the ability to get a Wi-Fi connection), pretty much anyone can set up a blog about pretty much anything. It's hugely unlikely that you'll write your blog in a completely empty niche. There will already be other people competing for your readers. If you want to build and keep an audience, you really need to stand out.

One way is to have a distinctive **identity** and **theme** for your content. We talked about using an angle to keep your enthusiasm high on a particular blog post. You can extend this to your whole blog to become an authority on a particular subject.

Look at what other people in your sector are writing about, and do something slightly different. You might be the person who focuses on the technical areas of a subject, or writes a regular roundup or digest of news on the subject. Whatever you do, you need to differentiate and create a reason for readers to visit you as well as other blogs in the same vertical.

Be regular
If you're blogging to build an audience and to help your search engine rankings, it's really important to keep a regular schedule of posting great content.

You should post a piece of rich content to the blog each week. By that I mean a piece of writing that adds value to the website and is something that your users will find useful and informative. On a regular basis you should create a plan of what you're going to post and when. Most blogging platforms like WordPress and Blogger allow you to schedule posts in advance, so you can do your writing at a time that's convenient for you, and publish it when your readers are most likely to be online.

Posting on a schedule gives readers something to expect, and you will find that if you post interesting things more regularly they will visit your site on more frequent basis to keep up with the latest information.

Remember that Google and Bing both value fresh content, and new pages will often rank pretty well straight away, and as such will help you get additional traffic from SEO.

Every page needs a purpose
As noted above, keeping to a schedule for content on your blog is really important, but something that's really important to remember is that there needs to be a reason to post. Nothing alienates your audience faster than pushing out content for the sake of having something new on the site.

Every piece of content that you post should have a purpose that is tied into your wider objectives for the blog.

If you're posting about something that's related to a specific product you sell, make sure you state that and include a call to action for your readers to find out more. If you're posting a news story, include your opinion on that story. Use the content to help potential customers understand more about your culture and what makes you different from the rest of the market.

Think about where the page you're writing fits into the way potential and existing customers interact with your brand and how you want them to act after they've read it.

Make Something Shareable

Every page you add to your website or blog needs to be there to add value to the user. When you're planning your content schedule, ask yourself the following questions:

- *Is this worth sharing?*
- *Would I share this with my friends*

If the answer is no, then don't bother posting.

Think in detail about why a person might share content from your website to other people in your chosen niche:

- *The content is highly informative*
- *The content is really funny*
- *The content is beautifully presented*
- *The content touches them*

One of the reasons why people share content with their social group online is that it will positively affect the way other people perceive them. If people think that sharing your content will make them look better, then they will share it.

Differentiate from other content
A symptom of a bad blog is a lot of content that is no different from what you'd see on any website in the same field. Pretty much every cycling blog will put out a post about riding carefully in winter, or what maintenance needs to be carried out on a bike. Why bother doing the same?

Remember what we said about having a unique angle for your blog?

People won't have a reason to come back to you unless you're doing something different from the crowd. Don't be afraid to do things differently – blogs can include things like video and images to complement your text. They're often more engaging for users, and more interesting too.

Think about the way your competitors describe something and try and do it differently. Concentrate on tighter niches in more detail when everyone is broad, and be broad when everyone else is narrow. Give people a reason to read your stuff rather than a competitor, and you'll be rewarded with more readers.

Use your voice
The way you write is your brand. Make sure that your style is recognisable to readers.

A lot of blogs – particularly blogs on company websites are pretty dry. That's often because too many restrictions are put on people expressing themselves properly. There are reasons for that: You don't want to undermine customer relationships, or have anything there that will harm the brand.

The downside of too much control over tone is that it ends up strangling the content and creating something that's so drab no-one will want to read it. A blog should be fairly casual. The content is designed to be consumed by people in a more relaxed way to a financial report or something like that.

You need to have some restraint (don't swear for example), but give your blog a voice. I have a friend who blogs for a city investment firm. He describes the writing style he uses as "taking his tie off". It's still smart, but a bit less formal. It works pretty well.

Encourage Participation

Whether you're writing a personal blog or acting as the mouthpiece for a company, a central part of a blog is community.

The worst thing you can do with a blog is to block comments. The second worst thing is to ignore them and not respond.

The content structure of a blog is more casual than a regular web page. If you write in a provocative way, or express an opinion on a particular topic, you should be open to the responses that you generate from it. Indeed, you should welcome them. A successful blog post isn't one that just gets a lot of views; a successful post is one that gets a lot of comments.

One of the things you need when blogging is a thick skin. The chances are that at some point a respondent will disagree, or be critical of what you've written. Expect to defend yourself, but stay true to your voice. Never post angry. If you do you risk turning the fighting rather than the writing into the reason someone visits your site.

Encourage Sharing

It's important to write something that people will want to share. That's how you build an audience. Of course you also need to encourage that sharing to happen. You can be subtle, or you can be explicit.

As a bare minimum, you should ensure that you have some sharing buttons for the most relevant social networks available on your website. If you're writing a business blog, you'll want LinkedIn alongside Facebook and Twitter.

You should also be comfortable asking for the share. That might be something soft like a note above your share buttons that says:

- *Please Share*

Or it might be something a little bit more explicit like:

- *Like what you've read? Share it*

Or even:

- *Did you enjoy this? Tell your friends.*

See what works best for you, and encourage users to follow the blog (or at least your Twitter account), so you can keep in touch.

Something I've tried (and it works) is to offer a free bonus to readers if they share – if you've bundled your best content into an eBook, you can give it away to people by letting them click through to a download page once they've liked or shared your post!

Track What Your Audience Like

One of the most important things that you can do to build your audience is to track what people like reading and are most likely to share and then do more of the same. If your readers like posts that take the form of a "top 10" list, then give them more.

The caveat to that is that you don't want to be the person who does the same thing every day. While certain posts might perform pretty well on a regular basis, that doesn't mean that you should avoid having some variety. After all, you want the blog to be something that becomes a long term relationship.

Doing the same thing over and over again will make you bored and pretty quickly you'll be running out of ideas. When you get bored, your writing will reflect that. Your posts will get sloppy and read like they've been phoned in. That will alienate your readers and they'll leave you. People who leave because they got bored ain't coming back.

Keep things fresh, but make sure you post enough of what works to ensure you get eyeballs on the stuff that really matters!

Be Brief When You Need to Be
Because there's no point using 10 words when 1 will do.

Posts that are long because they've not been edited – rather than being long because they need to be often drift. You've got limited time to engage a user. If your pages are unfocused and fluffy, people won't bother reading to the end. That means that they won't get to the part of the page where you ask them to share.

Write your post, go back over your post, edit your post. Take out anything unnecessary. Keep the writing tight, and don't be afraid to cut things. Just because you slaved over a really cool turn of phrase doesn't mean you need to keep it.

Tips for Email Marketing

As a business, your CRM data is one of your biggest assets, and email is a powerful weapon in marketing. It gives you an incredible opportunity to promote your business or services to an audience directly and without distractions.

When you're writing an email, the more you can tailor the experience to the individuals who will be reading it, the better. There are plenty of companies who will be able to analyse all of the data in your CRM, and provide you with different segments. That's important because it means at a general level you will be able to target content and offers to the people who are likely to be most receptive. Lists are valuable commodities, so don't waste them. If you're selling something, do everything you can to ensure that you have the right kind of people for the offer – otherwise, you'll burn the list fairly quickly and exhaust the opportunity of future sales. It's better to send an email to just 20 people and have 5 respond positively, than to send it to 100 and have 6, because the remainder of your contacts can still be approached in the future.

You should also consider where and when people will be reading your message. For the most part, we tend to access email on mobile devices these days. That means that your readers will see your message faster. It also means that they'll read it on a smaller screen, so bear that in mind when it comes to longer messages.

As a general rule, if you're sending an email, and the recipient is either not expecting it, or they don't know who you are, they'll treat it as spam and ignore it. With that in mind, you should do what you can to ensure that any emails you send are well timed, and most importantly, expected.

You need to be brief, polite, and honest in emails. Give the reader a clear message that they can understand and trust when scanning the first paragraph.

If you're sending business emails, measure everything and iterate. Test different subject lines, headings, and structure, look at how the audience reacts – use software that tracks statistics about open rate, response rate, and tally the data with your website analytics to get a full understanding of what works and what doesn't.

Killer Email Headings

Want to know the first step to a successful email marketing campaign?

It's simple. You get people to open your emails!

Unless your customers are actually opening the messages you send them, they can't read them, and if they don't read them, they won't find out about your offers.

If there's one thing that you absolutely have to get right in an email marketing campaign, it is your subject. That's the first thing that a reader sees in their inbox. Whether they're accessing your mail through Outlook on their desktop, or on their mobile phone, if the subject of the email doesn't pique their interest, they'll delete it.

Composing the subject of your email seems simple right? You're just going to tell people what's in the mail. Wrong! If you give all your secrets away without putting them in context (or surrounding them with the kind of persuasive messages that will help you sell), you're giving the reader less of an incentive to open the mail.

Here's some tips to help you get through the toughest part of the journey to email success: Writing killer email subjects that will make your readers click.

Intrigue the Reader

Let's be honest: if you're sending a sales email, a lot of the recipients don't want to receive it. As a result, they won't want to open it.

You need a title that will overcome their reluctance, and the easiest way of achieving that goal is to write something that's intriguing to them.

A lot of people mistake intrigue for being obscure, it's not. Intrigue is like a striptease where you reveal enough to excite, whereas obscurity is hiding so that you reveal nothing. People like intrigue, because it suggests excitement. They dislike a mask because it suggests something to fear:

- *Are you looking for something special?*

Is intriguing.

- *Open for more*

Is not.

Be Casual

A few years ago, the web was a bit more formal. Now, not so much. Because we chat so much on mobile devices and share content so freely, we're all a little bit more comfortable with being ourselves online. Sometimes too much so.

Casual and informal language is pretty much the norm online, and that's extended to email. We'd much rather say "Hi Dave" as an opening line than "Dear Mr Jones", and it's the same for subject lines.

Sales emails aren't always welcome, so you need to get through the initial reluctance of the recipient and make them open yours. An informal subject can often help with this:

- *Check out these offers*

Is casual enough to be from a friend, and it's a lot less intimidating than:

- *Save up to 25% with our latest discounts*

When you're writing your email subject, a good rule of thumb is "would I open this email". Hopefully you would answer "yes".

Just Say Hi

This is a variant on the ideas above, and was used to great effect during Barack Obama's election presidential election campaign where fundraising emails were sent out with the subject "Hey".

The reason this works is twofold.

Firstly, it says almost nothing. The recipient needs to open the email to find out what it is about, and provided you're able to follow through on your initial attraction, the chances are that you'll get them to read at least part of what you're offering.

The second reason why this is pretty effective is that it is the kind of email subject one friend would use to another. In a world of short form social media, where we communicate increasingly via one line of text, a short subject is exactly how we open a conversation.

One thing to bear in mind:

The reason this approach works pretty well is that it's not something that everyone does. The success Obama had means that you'll see this tip everywhere. The more people use it, the less recipients will trust it.

Use their name

If you're emailing someone, then you really should know their name. Otherwise, how can you say "Hi".

A person's name can be a powerful tool. It's one of their most prized possessions, and something that you can use to imply familiarity as part of your email. Most of the time, if you're sending out mass emails to potential customers, then you'll be using a mail merge of some kind to add some kind of personalization to the content of the email. Try personalizing the subject as well as your initial salutation:

- *Something special for Dave*
- *Hi Dave*
- *Looking for something to do this weekend Dave?*

Just be careful that the lines in your database match up and that your email software supports personalized titles. There's nothing more likely to get your mail ignored than getting the wrong name in the subject, or worse, having something like this:

- *Special Offers for [INSERTNAMEHERE]*

Be Conversational

There's a difference between casual and conversational. Casual language is language that's relaxed, and not intimidating. Being conversational is a bit more complex (but not much). What we're looking for is a statement that creates a dialogue between you and your reader, rather than a barrier.

Conversational email subjects are designed to elicit a response:

- *What's the next thing you're going to do?*

 Hopefully, open the email yeah?

Conversational email headers can be pretty useful, but as with all sales techniques, it's really important to think about what the response to a question will be. A question can be casual, intriguing and personal - all the things that we're trying to do with email subjects. It should also be the starting point for the whole of your email, and as such it's hugely important that you follow up on the question that you ask with an answer that makes sense and provides your reader with exactly what they expect.

Stand out

Every day I get about 200 emails. That doesn't take into account the ones that go straight into my spam folder, or the ones that my ISP picks up before they even get through to my account. Of those emails, I probably delete or ignore about 90% of the ones that aren't directly related to what I'm doing on a particular day.

Like most people, I'm time poor, and I have a pretty good filter system for things that don't stand out.

To get through that filter, an email needs to stand out. I need to want to read it above all the other things that appear in my inbox, and that's not easy to do.

Think about things that will catch the eye of your reader: We've talked about short casual titles, questions, and their name. Also think about numbers, symbols, and interesting words that are out of the ordinary.

AVOID CAPITAL LETTERS THOUGH. I DON'T WANT TO BE SHOUTED AT,

AND NEITHER DO YOUR READERS!

All Caps email subjects might stand out, but they're like the guy at the party who dances badly and wears a garish shirt. He might be tons of fun, but you wouldn't want to do anything aside from laugh at him.

Something to Think About

A key challenge for email providers is separating genuine emails from spam. They have black lists of words and senders that they use to filter email into the waste basket. Subjects that include terms like "money", "cheap" and "free" will often trigger the spam filter and mean that your carefully crafted email will not be seen by the target.

Write carefully and avoid any terms that might get you blocked.

Email Content Writing

Getting your reader to open the email is only half the battle. Then you've got to get them to read what you've sent them and ultimately encourage them to take the action that you want them to.

A good email will use many of the techniques that we talked about in the section on persuasive writing, but there's another consideration:

When you write a sales page on the web, your reader has generally chosen to visit it. They're there of their own accord, and as a result, they'll be that little bit more receptive to what you're offering. When you're selling via email, the most important thing you have to do is to get the reader on side as quickly as possible so that you put them into the kind of mind-set where they'll be open to what you have on offer and are more likely to take action.

Win over your reader

Your first priority when a reader opens the email you've sent is to win them over. This doesn't need to be hard work. It's about not making a mistake. You need to have a positive opening to the email that is tailored to the reader and gives them a bit of insight into what they're about to read.

Your opening needs to be three things:

- Personalised
- Polite
- Pleasing

You need to make the reader feel as though the email is for them (so get their name and salutation right).

You need to make the opening polite, thanking them for taking the time to read what you're saying.

You need to create a desire to learn more. The first paragraph needs to whet their appetite about what you're offering and how it's going to benefit them.

Avoid anything that seems either dishonest or exaggerated, and avoid writing in a stilted way. Don't be over familiar, or assume what they're thinking, because that will alienate the reader.

Also, keep the opening brief so that you don't waste the limited amount of time you've got your reader's attention for.

Hi Dave

I hope you're well. I wanted to reach out to you with some information about our offers. I think they'll be of interest.

Come to the point fast

Most of the time, a sales pitch is structured like this:

- *Tell the prospect what you're going to tell them*
- *Tell them*
- *Tell them what you've told them*

The longer you put off telling the reader what you've got on offer, the more likely they are to turn off, or click onto the next email in their inbox. Also, if you prevaricate, you run the risk of losing the reader's trust. People don't like to be teased, and they don't like to be kept waiting. Don't do either. As soon as you've finished the polite and personalised introduction, you want to move straight onto the appetizer:

> *I wanted to let you know about the launch of our new product. From next week it will be available in stores nationwide for $150, but as a special thank you for your support in the past, we're offering you the chance to get your hands on it early for just $125!*

Be brief

I wanted to send you a short email, but I didn't have time, so here's a long one.

Whether you're writing a novel or a tweet, as a writer, your duty is to communicate a set of ideas to another human being in the most economical way possible. That means using fewer words.

In the case of an email, it's vital that you get to the point quickly, but it's also essential that you complete your argument quickly too.

Don't mess about, and don't leave any unnecessary information. If you're selling via email, sell ONE thing not many. If I want to look at multiple products, I can visit your website. Concentrate on a single item for sale, and you'll find that the email gets a higher conversion rate.

Create a sense of urgency

One of the simplest and most effective ways of improving your chances of making a sale from an email is to create a sense of urgency for the reader. You can do this in two ways:

- *A limited number of items available*
- *A limited amount of time to benefit from a particular offer*

With both of these methods, you're essentially telling the reader if they don't act now, they'll miss out. As a result, it's important to let them know what the consequences of waiting are:

- *With only 5 items available, if you miss out today, you won't be able to order this in time for Christmas delivery.*

- *And remember, this is a limited time offer. Our 50% off sale ends on Wednesday.*

Be honest about the limits that you apply. Email marketing is advertising, and you are subject to standard advertising standards. If you say your offer ends on Thursday, it should.

Think about their objections

Just like a sales page, if you want your email to perform, you need to think about the objections your reader might have as they read the content and pre-emptively answer them. Your email should be simple, and to the point, giving the reader everything they need to know in order to take the next steps.

Unlike a face to face sale where you've got the opportunity to counter arguments as they're raised, in an email, you need to structure the content to handle the prospect effectively, giving them the reasons why they should buy rather than opportunities not to.

Read through your initial draft with another person and ask them where they are wandering. Address each point they raise but do it briefly. If a point needs explaining in more than a couple of lines, it generally means that the concept is too complex for an email sale, and you should concentrate on a different medium.

Use questions

A question is a pretty powerful tool isn't it?

When you address a reader with a question, you're inviting them to get more involved in a piece of text. Asking questions of the reader through your email will make it seem more personal to them than if you just assail them with statements.

The type of questions you ask need to be carefully structured into a conversation so that they flow from one to another covering off the various benefits of your product in order of importance.

How you present the questions is also important. Is it better to state the questions as sub-headings throughout the text, or expose them more subtly in the paragraphs of text? I prefer the latter, it makes the content flow more organically, but there are cases where you want to ask direct questions – especially when you're at the point of closing the sale in the text and you need to get your reader in the habit of saying yes.

... and answer them

A good sales email is a powerful piece of persuasive content that is brief but gives a reader all they need to know about what they're about to buy. We talked above about including questions throughout your copy to build a dialogue with the reader.

It's really important to answer the questions you ask – don't make your reader think unless it's about how to fill in the order form.

The big advantage of answering your questions is that you avoid the user bringing their doubts into the sale.

> What are you looking forward to most about your new motorbike? It's got to be the sense of freedom hasn't it? That sensation of getting out on the road on a sunny day and feeling the power. It's a great way to spend your weekend!

It can be tempting to leave a question up to the imagination of the reader. But in most cases, it's better not to. Don't leave things up to chance. You want people to think what you're thinking. Use a combination of open questions at the start of the email, and closed questions toward the end as you build commitment from the reader. Remember, you want the answers to be yes to get the reader in the habit of saying yes to the one question that matters at the end.

Include a call to action

So you've written a tight, well-structured email to a potential client. It's got just the right amount of information presented in an attractive way, and you've coached the reader to say yes. Getting all that spot on isn't easy, and it's all wasted if you don't remember to include a final call to action.

Think about what the most appropriate, and simplest next step for the customer is. Do you want them to call you, click through to the website to buy, or do you just want them to reply to the email?

Whatever the action required, make it as simple as possible to take the next steps. Make the call to action clear, and explain what will happen next:

> As soon as we receive your order, we'll give you a call to confirm the details, and your new items will be with you the next working day.
>
> [Buy Now]

Final Thoughts

Throughout this book, I've made the assumption that you as a reader are also a person who wants to write. You should, it's a rewarding process, and when you get it right, you have the opportunity to influence people in ways that benefit you both.

It's also a process that can be daunting, frustrating, and hard.

In business, customer interaction is an essential part of success. Getting your message right and presenting it in a way that your customers can engage with and understand easily is vital. If you find that you're struggling to write content that works for your business and customers, then find help.

If you decide to appoint a freelancer, spend time with them to help them understand your brand and customers. Give them the information they need to present your business as it is, rather than creating something that's vanilla and dull.

About the Author

This is me:

With more than a decade of experience in digital marketing, and a background in copywriting, I've worked with dozens of brands to help their businesses perform better online. I worked at one of the UK's largest digital marketing agencies and led the teams delivering Search Engine Optimisation and Content Strategy for brands like Wiggle, Hilton and Haven Holidays.

More recently I founded a consultancy business where I concentrate on working with clients to create holistic digital strategies covering content, social media and search marketing to help them find more clients.

Aside from this work, I've also written a book on SEO and am a regular speaker at conferences like SASCon where I tend to include pictures of cats in my slides.

If you'd like to find out more about what I do for businesses, drop me a line to James@compeller.co.uk, or find me on LinkedIn.

Mastering SEO:

The art and science of Search Engine Optimisation

This book covers the process of planning and executing an SEO strategy for businesses and includes specific information on technical optimisation of websites, keyword and audience research, and what to do if things go wrong.

It's a useful counterpoint to this book on writing for the web.

Writing for The Web

Made in the USA
Coppell, TX
23 March 2023

14657487R00039